LENT

COMPANION

LIFE TEEN

A special thanks to all those who have contributed to this resource in its original form.

Copy Editing by Natalie Tansill.

Cover Design by Casey Olson.
Interior Design by Laura Womack.

For more information about Life Teen or to order additional copies, go online to LifeTeen.com or call us at 1-800-809-3902.

TABLE OF CONTENTS

INTRODUCTION

When you ask most Catholics about Lent you'll probably be told about how we're not supposed to eat meat on Fridays or how we're supposed to give up foods and drinks that we love. You might even hear about how we're not supposed to say the "A" word at Mass (you know, the one that rhymes with "shmalleluia"). Obviously, though, if that's all there was to Lent we wouldn't have taken the time to put together this book, and the Church wouldn't go to all the trouble she does encouraging us to make some bigger changes in our lives.

Lent doesn't exactly get the same response that Advent does. Think about it.

During Advent, everyone's happy. They're anticipating Christmas, hanging decorations and buying gifts. Christmas music is everywhere and the Christmas story about the beautiful baby in the manger is shared across the globe. Even people who don't believe Christ is God share the "Christmas Spirit." The season is immersed in love and in giving, which is a thoroughly "Christian" message, right?

During Lent, however, people's moods aren't quite as "jolly." We begin by smearing ashes on our foreheads and proclaiming that we're sinners. We try to eliminate bad habits, give up (usually unhealthy) things we have grown to enjoy, we abstain from meat, and we fast. The story doesn't "end" with a baby in a manger but, rather, a carpenter on a cross. The message of the empty tomb, for many, is as fictional as an egg-delivering bunny. The season of Lent is immersed in death, paving the way for new life... which is also a thoroughly Christian message, though not as popular.

It's no wonder that so many souls — even souls who go to Mass every Sunday — prefer Advent to Lent, but the truth is that we need both. You can't separate the manger from the cross. Jesus was born to die so that we would live. Christ came so that we would learn what (and more to the point, Who) love really is (1 John 4:8). And true love requires sacrifice.

Lent is more than just a season before Easter. Lent is a forty-day journey for your mind, body, and soul. Our souls can direct our minds. Our minds influence what we do with our bodies. What we do with our minds and bodies have an effect on our souls. They're all interconnected; the question is whether your soul leads your body or whether your body leads your soul. Lent is a great time to make sure that our souls, minds, and bodies are working in the right order.

That's one reason why we spend an entire season looking at our lives: where we've come from, where we are, and where we are going. This time of reflection often reveals the need to change some things and to repent for our sins.

WHAT IT MEANS TO REPENT

When we repent for a sin we express sincere regret, and even remorse, for what we did. To repent, or to be "penitent," means that you not only realize and admit the reality and effects of sin in your life, but that you also sincerely want to stop that sin, turn away from it, and conquer it with the help of God's grace.

Repenting is an action, not just a thought. It's deciding to go 180 degrees in the other direction. It's like a spiritual U-turn. You'll notice that when you go forward to receive ashes on Ash Wednesday, the prayer often uttered as the ashes are placed upon your forehead is, *"Turn away from sin, and return to the gospel"* (Mark 1:15).

The first action of **repentance**, the "turning away from sin," is a ninety-degree movement to the right. You are no longer trapped by sin... but merely turning ninety degrees has left you "better off," but not free. It's in the next ninety degrees that we fully comprehend **repentance**. The second action is a "returning to the Gospel." It's in this movement that we forsake the lies and the false securities of the sin and turn completely away from the darkness. It's in this movement that we face God's magnificent light with our whole existence. Now, this full 180-degree movement of **repentance** is not easy.[1]

Repentance requires humility and sincerity, and often sacrifice. As you know, during Lent we are challenged to make sacrifices in our lives. The sacrifices can be big or small and are supposed to help us grow in holiness.

WHY DO WE SACRIFICE?

Have you ever wondered why we "sacrifice" things to God anyway? Have you ever asked why God wants us to sacrifice to Him?

Since God is the Creator of all things, it means that absolutely everything is a gift from the Creator: every drop of rain, blade of grass, piece of fruit, animal, and person.

"When God asks us, His creation, for a sacrifice — like an animal in Abel's case — it's not because He needs it. God doesn't need food. He asks us because we need it. We, as His creation, need to remember WHOM our blessings come from. We need to show the Creator that we love Him more than the things He created. By sacrificing things back to Him, we not only show our reliance on God, but we also show

[1] Mark Hart, *The 'R' Father: 14 Ways to Respond to the Lord's Prayer* (Ijamsville, Maryland: Word Among Us Press, 2010), 135.

Him that we are more in love with the One who gives us the blessings than we are with the blessings themselves."[2]

"There is nothing you can do to make God love you more. And there is nothing you can do to make God love you less. He loves you perfectly. Going to church doesn't make God love you more. Rather, going to church helps us to love God and our brothers and sisters in Christ more. Praising God doesn't make God love you more. Rather, praising God helps us to focus less on ourselves and more on God. Serving the poor, giving money (tithing) to the Church, resisting temptation and sin, fasting or making other sacrifices doesn't make God love you more. But it does please Him, since all of those things help us to grow in love and become more like Christ."[3]

Lent is not only a time to give things up but also to "add things on"; a time to spend more time and put more energy into prayer, acts of service, spiritual reading, exercise, and other activities that will help us grow in both healthiness and holiness.

[2] Mark Hart, *"Finding Yourself in Scripture"* (Mesa, Arizona: Life Teen, 2010), 4.
[3] Ibid., 5

HOW TO USE THIS BOOK

This Lent Companion is meant to be just that — a companion for you during your Lenten journey into the spiritual desert. If you're reading this book, you're obviously taking ownership of your spiritual growth and that pleases God. Your spiritual life could change dramatically over the next several weeks if you allow the Holy Spirit to lead you.

The reflections and ideas within this booklet should serve as a starting point for your Lent, but not the ending point. You might find this Companion most helpful if you "journal" daily or weekly as you go along. Journaling is simply a written record of your dialogue with God. When you journal as a form of prayer, you are expressing your thoughts (or more specifically, the movements of your heart) in writing instead of through speaking or silence.

The only rule to journaling is that there are no rules. Over time you can go back to see what you've written on the pages (and later, the filled journals). You'll be amazed not only at how your life and your perspective change over time, but by how faithful God is to you, both daily and eternally. He will not let you down, ever. He is waiting for you. Go to Him in prayer.

Scripture promises us, "Draw near to God and He will draw near to you" (James 4:8), and Lent is the perfect time to do that.

Once you've spent some time in silence and in prayer, just start writing. You can journal as long or as briefly as you feel inspired to do. Some days you might journal for an hour or more. Other days you might write one sentence or nothing at all. Neither the days of filled pages, nor those of empty pages should ever be viewed as a failure; anytime you put yourself in the presence of God and listen is a success.

In addition to journaling, here are a few more ideas on how to "get the most" out of each section:

SCRIPTURE PASSAGE

Each Gospel reading is taken directly from the Gospel for that day's Mass. Try to read and pray through the passage a few times prior to going to Mass. You'll be amazed at how much more you get out of the liturgy. Make it a point, as well, to look for details, adjectives, and other descriptive words that bring the story to life. Underline key words or phrases that jump out at you and write out any questions that you may have, so that you can ask them later.

REFLECTION

The Scripture readings are deep and there is a lot you can take from each of them. These reflections are intended to start your brain and heart moving in the same direction. After reading the reflection spend some time journaling about it or discussing what you read, as well as sharing your own thoughts with friends, family, or with others from the Church.

A PERSONAL CHALLENGE

There are thoughts included for every day of the week to better live out and enter into the themes and readings discussed prior. Some might need to be adapted to your specific age, vocation, and life, but use these as practical ideas that you can implement and build upon. Be intentional. Do something every day to enter more deeply into the Lenten season.

ASH
WEDNESDAY

ASH WEDNESDAY

MARCH 5, 2014

READING I
Joel 2:12-18

READING II
2 Corinthians 5:20 - 6:2

GOSPEL
Jesus said to his disciples:

"Take care not to perform righteous deeds in order that people may see them; otherwise, you will have no recompense from your heavenly Father. When you give alms, do not blow a trumpet before you, as the hypocrites do in the synagogues and in the streets to win the praise of others. Amen, I say to you, they have received their reward. But when you give alms, do not let your left hand know what your right is doing, so that your almsgiving may be secret. And your Father who sees in secret will repay you.

When you pray, do not be like the hypocrites, who love to stand and pray in the synagogues and on street corners so that others may see them. Amen, I say to you, they have received their reward. But when you pray, go to your inner room, close the door, and pray to your Father in secret. And your Father who sees in secret will repay you.

When you fast, do not look gloomy like the hypocrites. They neglect their appearance, so that they may appear to others to be fasting. Amen, I say to you, they have received their reward. But when you fast, anoint your head and wash your face, so that you may not appear to be fasting, except to your Father who is hidden. And your Father who sees what is hidden will repay you."

- Matthew 6:1-6, 16-18

REFLECTION

Lent is a season that calls us to a renewed relationship with Christ through prayer, almsgiving, and fasting. Today's Gospel provides us with a reality check as Lent begins: Are we doing those things for Christ or are we "living for the applause"?

It can be difficult to "not blow a trumpet" after we do a good deed. Okay, you may not have a trumpet — but you do have a Twitter, Instagram, or Facebook account. Are you posting about the service night you just participated in for affirmation or to glorify God?

Are you giving something up for Lent as a way to show people how holy you are? Are you ramping up the difficulty because you want to grow closer to Christ by removing something in your life to focus on Him, or so people can admire how spiritually "mature" you are for taking on such a challenge?

How many times today do you plan on complaining of hunger to your friends and family? Are you going to make sure your Twitter followers know you are fasting and how hard it is?

Jesus asks us to avoid such behaviors and instead do them in secret. By fasting, but not allowing others to know we are fasting, by praying in secret, and by doing good deeds that no one can see, we do those things truly for God and for others in a selfless way. It makes Lent less about us and what we are going to do and more about our relationship with God and what He wants to do for us.

This Lent, don't make it about the applause or affirmation. Make it about Christ and what He is going to do in your life, if you let Him.

A PERSONAL CHALLENGE

Commit to a daily routine of prayer and an aspect of fasting, and at least one weekly act of service or almsgiving. Don't tell anyone what they are, and strive to do them in secret for the rest of Lent.

THURSDAY AFTER ASH WEDNESDAY

MARCH 6, 2014

GOSPEL
Luke 9:22-25

REFLECTION

In this Gospel passage, Christ makes clear the suffering that He will go through. He tells His apostles that He will suffer greatly and be rejected, but that He would rise (from the dead) on the third day. So, although He will die on the cross, He foretold the Resurrection through prophecy. He reminded them that His death would not be the end.

So many people wrongly think that following Christ is a "piece of cake" — but Christ, Himself, made it clear that for those that follow Him, suffering will not be far. But, the suffering that Christ went through was not pointless — it led to salvation.

We are called to follow in Jesus' footsteps — and Christ makes it clear, in this Gospel, that those who wish to enter the Kingdom of God will need to take up their cross and follow Him.

A PERSONAL CHALLENGE

Write out a list of things that you have been complaining about recently, whether it's the weather or an annoying situation. Choose to not voice those complaints, but instead when you feel the urge to complain out loud, offer it up to God by praying a decade of the Rosary.

FRIDAY AFTER ASH WEDNESDAY

MARCH 7, 2014

GOSPEL
Matthew 9:14-15

REFLECTION

Wedding celebrations are full of love, joy, and excitement. Who doesn't love a good feast and the chance to celebrate with the bride and bridegroom? In today's Gospel passage, Jesus calls Himself the bridegroom and His disciples the wedding guests. He is reminding us of the huge blessing it is that He is with us. God is truly always with us! Do we remember that? Do we see and appreciate that as the gift that it is?

On the other hand, Jesus also reminds the people that He, the bridegroom, will not always be with them (physically, as He was when He walked on earth). We are especially aware throughout this season of the apparent absence of Christ — the absence of the bridegroom. As the bridegroom, Jesus sacrificed so much for His bride, the Church. As we begin this Lenten season, we fast, pray, and sacrifice to remember all that Jesus gave up for us.

A PERSONAL CHALLENGE

What is one way you can intentionally remember Jesus' sacrifice on the cross for you more regularly? Commit to doing something today that will not only help you better appreciate His sacrifice, but will help you remember it more often.

SATURDAY AFTER ASH WEDNESDAY

MARCH 8, 2014

GOSPEL
Luke 5:27-32

REFLECTION

We cannot share what we don't possess. But if we know Christ, we are called to get out of our comfort zone — our circle of friends — and share Christ to those who may have never heard of Him. Our faith is not meant to be kept to ourself. Our faith should be like an overflowing bucket; so much love welling up that it's spilling out and overflowing onto others. Sharing our faith then becomes a natural impulse and not a chore.

Often times we are guilty of making surface judgments as to who might be open to the Gospel and we avoid particular types of people. It can be easy to avoid sharing our Faith with those who seem too cool for God, those who may annoy us, or those who seem to be satisfied with living in sin. But those who seem most different from us are often the ones hungering for God the most. We need the courage to share Christ with others, even if they might reject us. As their rejection is between themselves and God.

Our words don't have to be profound. Christ just said, "Follow me," and that was enough to captivate new followers.

A PERSONAL CHALLENGE

Next time you're next to a stranger in a coffee shop, in line at the grocery store, or on an airplane, say a quick prayer for them and ask that God would open them up for a conversation. If God wants you to evangelize, He'll open the doors.

FIRST WEEK
OF LENT

FIRST SUNDAY OF LENT

MARCH 9, 2014

READING I
Genesis 2:7-9; 3:1-7

READING II
Romans 5:12-19 or Romans 5:12, 17-19

GOSPEL

At that time Jesus was led by the Spirit into the desert to be tempted by the devil. He fasted for forty days and forty nights, and afterwards he was hungry. The tempter approached and said to him, "If you are the Son of God, command that these stones become loaves of bread." He said in reply, "It is written: One does not live on bread alone, but on every word that comes forth from the mouth of God." Then the devil took him to the holy city, and made him stand on the parapet of the temple, and said to him, "If you are the Son of God, throw yourself down. For it is written: He will command his angels concerning you and with their hands they will support you, lest you dash your foot against a stone." Jesus answered him, "Again it is written, You shall not put the Lord, your God, to the test."

Then the devil took him up to a very high mountain, and showed him all the kingdoms of the world in their magnificence, and he said to him, "All these I shall give to you, if you will prostrate yourself and worship me." At this, Jesus said to him, "Get away, Satan! It is written: The Lord, your God, shall you worship and him alone shall you serve."

Then the devil left him and, behold, angels came and ministered to him.

- Matthew 4:1-11

REFLECTION

Jesus Christ draws near to us in all things, even in dealing with temptations. Christ fasted for forty days and forty nights while He was in the desert. And although He was hungry and tempted by the devil, He remained strong in His resistance of the temptation. The fact that He fasted is important because it ensured that His soul led His body, rather than His body leading His soul. The strength He gained through His fasting strengthened Him for the temptations that followed. This reveals to us not only the necessity of fasting, but its power in the spiritual realm. That is why fasting is such a pivotal part of Lent, it is our own forty days to fast with Christ as we continue to fight the devil and the sins and temptations in our lives.

Throughout this passage two very important things are happening: Jesus Christ is overcoming major temptations that all mankind faces and He is fighting the devil through the power of the Word of God. It is incredible to see the power of Jesus, for even in the most extreme of circumstances He never falters and gives in to the temptations of the Devil.

So where does Christ's strength come from? Yes, He is the Son of God, but He also uses Scripture as He fights against the devil. The first thing we can learn is that the Word of God truly is "sharper than any two-edged sword" (Hebrews 4:12). It is through knowledge of the Scriptures that Christ is able to battle Satan in His greatest moments of temptation. Even in the midst of temptation, Christ offers us a model of how to overcome temptation. He shows us not only the power that the Scriptures hold but also how they can help us overcome any sort of temptation. God gives us the words to say when we are in need, and the words to say that will make the devil leave us alone, we just need to do our part to learn these Words of God.

The second thing that this passage shows us is that Satan is very smart, and he will do everything in his power to make us falter, including fighting against us by twisting the truth. Not only is Christ using Scripture in this passage, but Satan is too. So we must always be on our guard, we need to know the Word of God, and most importantly we need a relationship with Christ so that we can understand His words. In times of temptation, we need to draw on all our weapons including the Scriptures but also the strength and grace of God that comes to us through the sacraments and prayer.

A PERSONAL CHALLENGE

What is one main sin or temptation that you continuously struggle with? Commit to overcoming that temptation with Christ. Put the Scripture passage below on post-it notes around your house, on your books, or in your car, and use the Word of God along with the Sacrament of Reconciliation to fight these struggles in your life.

"Because he himself was tested through what he suffered, he is able to help those who are being tested" (Hebrews 2:18).

MONDAY

GOSPEL
Matthew 25:31-46

REFLECTION

It is so easy to simply ignore those who are in need around us. Perhaps where you live there aren't a lot of hungry or homeless people. Because of that, it can be easy to think that there aren't people in need or that they are only found in foreign countries or big cities. However, that couldn't be further from the truth. Blessed Mother Teresa of Calcutta reminds us that we do not have to travel to a foreign country or to the inner city to find people who need help. There are people who are spiritually hungry or homeless sitting right next to us in class, on the bus, in the cafeteria, or even at our dinner table.

Jesus isn't asking us to do something extraordinary in this Gospel. He is simply asking us to care about those around us and to be aware of the needs of others and not ignore them. When we love those who are broken, abandoned, hurting, or lonely, we are not just loving them, but loving Jesus who is present with them in their suffering.

Don't only be concerned about yourself, completely oblivious to the world around you. Instead, be led by the Good Shepherd and attentive to His voice, ready to bring others close to Him so that they may be healed and restored.

A PERSONAL CHALLENGE

Make it a point to love someone around you who is ignored or hurting by going out of your way to talk to them on the way to class or eat lunch with them. Pray for them as well, asking that you may be an instrument of Jesus' love in their life.

TUESDAY

MARCH 11, 2014

GOSPEL

Matthew 6:7-15

REFLECTION

Prayer is one of the most important parts of our faith — prayer literally is our relationship with God. While Christ was on earth, He modeled for us how we should pray. He showed us that prayer goes beyond just saying words.

In this passage, He gave us the Our Father. He taught us how to pray; and since He is God, this is something not to be taken lightly. He wants us to have a relationship with our Father in heaven — and this passage is where Christ shows us how that relationship grows. Notice the "order" to the prayer... it's about God before it's about us.

A PERSONAL CHALLENGE

Take some time today to journal about the Our Father. Write out the prayer on a piece of paper and then underline phrases that stick out to you. Then, ask God why those particular phrases stuck out and journal about them.

WEDNESDAY

MARCH 12, 2014

GOSPEL
Luke 11:29-32

REFLECTION
In our increasingly visual culture with iPhones and Instagram it seems normal to ask for some proof if someone is making a big claim. We need a "sign" if we are supposed to truly believe what we are hearing.

In our prayer and when we struggle with doubt, we can be tempted to ask God for a sign to let us know that He is truly there.

But this mindset can lead to a big problem. Sometimes we can be so focused on a big "sign" from God to answer our prayers that we can become oblivious to the way Christ is working in our lives on a day-to-day basis. In this passage, the people were looking for Jesus to provide "proof" through a big miracle or sign, but we know that Jesus coming to earth, dying on the cross, and being resurrected is the "sign" that brings us eternal life.

A PERSONAL CHALLENGE

This week, ask God to help you see small blessings in your own life that teach you more about Him and His love for you.

THURSDAY

GOSPEL
Matthew 7:7-12

REFLECTION

Initially while reading this passage it may seem like God will always answer our prayers just the way we hope He will. But even in this passage it's unclear as to whether they received exactly what they were asking or looking for. The truth is that as much as we want God to answer our prayer exactly the way we think He should, that is not how prayer works.

The passage compares the heavenly Father to a parent giving his child what the child desires. But if a child asked a parent to eat candy for every meal of the day, would a good, loving parent allow that child to actually live on candy alone? While a young child may not understand the problem with his request, out of love, a good parent gives his child what the child truly needs. Our heavenly Father treats us in the same way. While we may be discouraged when He doesn't answer our prayer in the way we want Him to, we should be encouraged knowing that out of His great love for us and in His great wisdom, He is bestowing blessings upon us in exactly the way we need.

A PERSONAL CHALLENGE

Think about a time in your life when God answered a prayer differently than you had expected and how, in hindsight, the situation turned out far better than you could have imagined. Take some time to journal about that experience.

FRIDAY

MARCH 14, 2014

GOSPEL
Matthew 5:20-26

REFLECTION

Jesus teaches us in this Gospel passage that the commandments are not just to be taken at face value. He tells us that "to kill" is not only to not murder. Through our anger and the effects of anger — grudges, hatred, abuse — we can also break this commandment. To never kill is one thing, but this commandment is about more than murder. Christ is telling us that it's not about the letter of the law — taking the commandment literally — but rather, it's about the spirit of the law.

The spirit of the law goes much deeper than the letter of the law. Christ was not just telling people to obey the commandments, but to get to the heart of the law. Ultimately, Jesus is calling us to love. A heart full of anger or bound by grudges cannot also be filled with the love of Christ. We may never outwardly harm, but even to have anger, hatred, and grudges in our hearts will keep us from the righteousness necessary to enter heaven.

A PERSONAL CHALLENGE

When something, or someone upsets you today, say a prayer of blessing and ask for God's grace for the person or situation.

SATURDAY

MARCH 15, 2014

GOSPEL

Matthew 5:43-48

REFLECTION

"So be perfect, just as your heavenly Father is perfect" (Matthew 5:48). No big deal, right? While reading this passage it is easy to see it as just some lofty goal that no one ever really achieves. But if we pray with

this passage we come to experience a much deeper reality.

Christ never gives us a command or challenge that is impossible. In fact, Jesus constantly gives us the road map to making holy decisions in our journey towards heaven. This is one of those times. Perfection is not something that comes through having the perfect body, the best car, the best looking boyfriend or girlfriend, or even from being in the top ten percent of your class. Perfection comes from loving your enemies and demonstrating forgiveness to those who cross your path. When we choose to love an enemy and show them mercy, we share in the very mission of Jesus Christ. We become Christ in those moments and we bring perfection into an imperfect and broken world. So be perfect... love your enemies and show them forgiveness.

A PERSONAL CHALLENGE

Set aside a time today to pray a Divine Mercy chaplet specifically for someone who you have a hard time forgiving. Try to reflect on how that person is a child of God the Father, the same as you.

SECOND WEEK
OF LENT

SECOND SUNDAY OF LENT

MARCH 16, 2014

READING I
Genesis 12:1-4a

READING II
2 Timothy 1:8b-10

GOSPEL

Jesus took Peter, James, and John his brother, and led them up a high mountain by themselves. And he was transfigured before them; his face shone like the sun and his clothes became white as light. And behold, Moses and Elijah appeared to them, conversing with him. Then Peter said to Jesus in reply, "Lord, it is good that we are here. If you wish, I will make three tents here, one for you, one for Moses, and one for Elijah." While he was still speaking, behold, a bright cloud cast a shadow over them, then from the cloud came a voice that said, "This is my beloved Son, with whom I am well pleased; listen to him." When the disciples heard this, they fell prostrate and were very much afraid.

But Jesus came and touched them, saying, "Rise, and do not be afraid." And when the disciples raised their eyes, they saw no one else but Jesus alone.

As they were coming down from the mountain, Jesus charged them, "Do not tell the vision to anyone until the Son of Man has been raised from the dead."

- Matthew 17:1-9

REFLECTION

In this story of the Transfiguration of Jesus, we hear about how Jesus revealed His divine glory to three of His apostles. What an awesome moment for those apostles! Can you imagine? They were getting a glimpse of the glory of heaven and their faith was strengthened by the knowledge that this man was indeed the Son of God. That's an amazing gift, right? It's no wonder that Peter offered to pitch some tents so they could stay there and enjoy this happy, heavenly reunion.

But that moment of bliss was only supposed to be for a short time. There was still much work to be done, and much suffering to be endured before they could partake in the glory of heaven and be free from the pain of the world. It's a perfectly natural reaction to want to skip out on the cross and jump right to the eternal prize. Aren't we guilty of the same thing?

Don't we regret going home after an amazing retreat experience? Don't we sometimes wish we could stay in the peace of the chapel instead of going out into the messiness of the world? Don't we long for moments of consolation and comfort from God rather than trials and sufferings that test our faith?

You can't become a saint without being purified through the fire of suffering. All the struggles that we go through, all the times we feel distant from God, or all the muck of the world that we have to deal with can be used to make us holier people. God loves us too much to let us stay comfortable in an exciting experience of His glory. Those times are gifts, but they can't be the expected norm.

Just like Peter, James, and John, we have to come down from the mountaintop. We have to get back to our lives after a moment of glory. But the good news is that Jesus comes with us. He could remain distant, in unapproachable light... but that's not the kind of God we have. We have a God who knows when to strengthen our faith with moments of great grace and when we need to be challenged by the cross. May we have the grace to embrace both.

A PERSONAL CHALLENGE

Think about a time when God gave you the gift of a glorious moment when you truly felt His presence and His glory. Journal about that time and thank God for it. Keep that account and try to remember to look back on it when you're struggling to carry your cross or can't feel God's presence. Ask for the grace to remember that God always has your best interest in mind — whether in times of glory or times of trial.

MONDAY

MARCH 17, 2014

GOSPEL
Luke 6:36-38

REFLECTION

This Gospel may sound like it's pretty easy enough to handle, but to actually live out what this Gospel is telling us takes practice.

For this passage is really calling us to be like our Father in heaven, who is perfect. We are called to show others mercy and love, because that's what God does for us. Since we are made in the image

and likeness of God, we are called to be like Him.
Since God forgives, we should forgive. Since God is
generous, we should be generous. Because God loves
us, we should love others.

There may be people in your life that you need to
forgive or people that may be hard to love, but this
Gospel sets the standard high. God forgives and
He loves unconditionally, no matter what. Be like
Christ... choose to love and choose to forgive.

A PERSONAL CHALLENGE
Make it a point to forgive someone that has hurt you
and pray that they may find Christ's joy today.

TUESDAY

MARCH 18, 2014

GOSPEL
Matthew 23:1-12

REFLECTION
The Pharisees and the teachers of the law made
themselves the model of how to act. They put the
focus on themselves and all the external things that

people "needed" to do in order to be righteous. However, with all the emphasis on the external aspects of the law, they neglected the internal part of the law — the heart. Jesus calls them out in this Gospel for placing the hard tasks on others and doing everything for attention. Jesus warns them against hypocrisy.

It can be very tempting to want people to recognize you for the good things that you do — and it can be disheartening when no one notices or compliments you for something good you've done. But instead of looking for the recognition or attention from others, remember that God sees all that you do. As Scripture reminds us, "Whoever exalts himself will be humbled; but whoever humbles himself will be exalted" (Matthew 23:12).

Jesus is our perfect example of humility, freely dying upon the cross for our sins, taking away our burden and carrying it Himself. We must strive for humility by the grace of God so that the only one we seek approval from is our heavenly Father.

A PERSONAL CHALLENGE
Find a way today to do a random act of service for somebody without anyone knowing it was you.

WEDNESDAY

GOSPEL
Mathew 1:16, 18-21, 24a or Luke 2:41-51a

REFLECTION
Why did God choose St. Joseph? Why him and not some other man? What were the attributes that God saw within him, that made him the guy God chose to model manliness to His only Son, Jesus.

For that matter, why did Mary need a husband at all? Couldn't God have assigned Mary a couple of extra guardian angels to help her as a single mother? Wouldn't that have been an incredible example, too? Why "mess up" the really holy combination of Jesus and Mary with a sinner like Joseph? Obviously, God's plan was bigger. St. Joseph wasn't just there as divinely-inspired "window dressing" to make the holy family a little "less perfect" and more relatable. In St. Joseph we have a model of holiness, virtue, and quiet strength. We never even hear St. Joseph speak, but his actions speak far louder than words. He sought the will of God over his own desires. He sought Mary's protection over his own reputation. He was obedient to God at every moment of human confusion and indecision. His fidelity and trust are examples that God desperately wanted us to have and that the Holy Spirit saw to it were recorded — forever — in Sacred Scripture.

A PERSONAL CHALLENGE

On a blank piece of paper, write the phrase, "God, I refuse to trust You with..." and then write a list of each of those things you struggle to let God be the Lord of in your life like your vocation, your future, your relationships, your stress, your family, your struggles or addictions or doubts. Then spend some time in prayer and invite the Lord to take that struggle from you. Ask the Lord to help you to trust more and cross out each one that you feel He is calling you to give to Him. Ask St. Joseph to pray with you throughout this prayerful exercise.

THURSDAY

MARCH 20, 2014

GOSPEL
Luke 16:19-31

REFLECTION

After reading this passage, the first thought we might have is: *If you have a good life here on earth,*

you'll suffer later, and if you are suffering now you are
assured of getting to heaven.

We know that is not how it works. What matters is
how we live our faith and one way to do that is to
respond to God's call to care for the poor.

The rich man ignored the suffering of Lazarus. How
often do we ignore situations where we could help
others?

There are many ways a person can be poor and many
ways one can be wealthy. We all have needs so we are
all poor in some way. But we all have many gifts too.
Some can give financially, others through service in
their church, family or community and all of us can
offer prayers.

During Lent, the Church encourages us to think less
about ourselves and more about others. If we do this,
we will no longer be able to ignore the poor as the
rich man did. Jesus said "Truly I tell you, whatever
you did for one of the least of these brothers and
sisters of mine, you did for me" (Matthew 25:40).

A PERSONAL CHALLENGE

Blessed Teresa of Calcutta was an excellent example
of someone that served the poorest of the poor. Read
about her life and decide how you will serve Christ in
the poor today.

FRIDAY

MARCH 21, 2014

GOSPEL
Matthew 21:33-43, 45-56

REFLECTION
Greed and personal gain are taking over our society. The constant want for more is ruining our relationship with the Lord. There may have been moments in our life where we give in to temptation and we may have beaten another person with our words, or stoned them with our actions so we could gain a higher position in our school or work place.

The Lord is commanding us to stop. We have the choice to either use our gifts for God's glory or not. Christ gave us the gifts so that we can honor Him, so when we look at the gifts that others have and think, "I want that" or "I wish I had that," we fail to see the blessings God gives us. Instead look at your gifts and offer them up to Jesus today. Don't hold back. You are wonderfully and perfectly made in His eyes.

A PERSONAL CHALLENGE
Write a list of all the gifts you have been given by the Lord. Journal about a way that you will use those gifts to glorify the Kingdom, then go out and do just that.

SATURDAY

MARCH 22, 2014

GOSPEL
Luke 15:1-3, 11-32

REFLECTION

In this Gospel passage, Jesus tells the parable of the Prodigal Son. The great thing about this parable is that we can find ourselves in the characters. Are we the one who left the father or the one who stays? The father in the parable is a great example of the unfailing, unconditional love of our Father in heaven. Have you ever stopped and reflected on how incredibly loving the father is?

First of all, the father sees him from far away and only has compassion for him. No matter how far you feel from God today, He is looking toward you with only compassion.

Secondly, the father ran to his son. God is not a passive God, but a God who is pursuing us, yes — even running toward us. If you want to find God, just stop running from Him. Because God is always pursuing us, it won't take long for Him to reach us.

Thirdly, the father in the parable doesn't dwell on the past but rather, celebrates the present time. How often do we mess up thinking that God is keeping score even after we receive the Sacrament of Reconciliation? God has forgiven us and celebrates us; can we forgive ourselves and live in the present?

However you view God, if your view doesn't include a compassionate, pursuing, and celebrating over you God, you're missing out.

A PERSONAL CHALLENGE

Today write a letter from God to you. Simply take a blank piece of paper and start writing whatever God places in your head and heart. The first couple of lines might sound like they are coming from you but keep writing. After awhile you won't believe all that He wants to tell you!

THIRD WEEK
OF LENT

THIRD SUNDAY OF LENT

MARCH 23, 2014

READING I
Exodus 17:3-7

READING II
Romans 5:1-2, 5-8

GOSPEL

Jesus came to a town of Samaria called Sychar, near the plot of land that Jacob had given to his son Joseph. Jacob's well was there. Jesus, tired from his journey, sat down there at the well. It was about noon.

A woman of Samaria came to draw water. Jesus said to her, "Give me a drink." His disciples had gone into the town to buy food. The Samaritan woman said to him, "How can you, a Jew, ask me, a Samaritan woman, for a drink?" — For Jews use nothing in common with Samaritans. — Jesus answered and said to her, "If you knew the gift of God and who is saying to you, 'Give me a drink,' you would have asked him and he would have given you living water." The woman said to him, "Sir, you do not even have a bucket and the cistern is deep; where then can you get this living water? Are you greater than our father Jacob, who gave us this cistern and drank from it himself with his children and his flocks?" Jesus answered and said to her, "Everyone who drinks this water will be thirsty again; but whoever drinks the water I shall give will never thirst; the water I shall give will become in him a spring of water welling up to eternal life." The woman said to him, "Sir, give me this water, so that I may not be thirsty or have to keep coming here to draw water.

"I can see that you are a prophet. Our ancestors worshiped on this mountain; but you people say that the place to worship is in Jerusalem." Jesus said to her, "Believe me, woman, the hour is coming when you will worship the Father neither on this mountain nor in Jerusalem. You people worship what you do not understand; we worship what we understand, because salvation is from the Jews. But the hour is coming, and is now here, when true worshipers will worship the Father in Spirit and truth; and indeed the Father seeks such people to worship him. God is Spirit, and those who worship him must worship in Spirit and truth." The woman said to him, "I know that the Messiah is coming, the one called the Christ; when he comes, he will tell us everything." Jesus said to her, "I am he, the one who is speaking with you."

Many of the Samaritans of that town began to believe in him. When the Samaritans came to him, they invited him to stay with them; and he stayed there two days. Many more began to believe in him because of his word, and they said to the woman, "We no longer believe because of your word; for we have heard for ourselves, and we know that this is truly the savior of the world."

- John 4:5-15, 19b-26, 39a, 40-42

REFLECTION

This Sunday's Gospel reading is about a Samaritan woman and the interaction that Jesus has with her. But this interaction with the Samaritan woman can be viewed like our relationship with God: He knows us, He knows what we need, and He is what we need.

As Jesus meets the Samaritan woman, we begin to realize that this isn't just some normal interaction. Men and woman of this time and culture don't talk to each other like this (unless they are married). Nor do Jews (Jesus and disciples) and Samaritans interact like this. And this is sort of alarming to the Samaritan woman. How often do we think God doesn't know everything about us? How often do we act surprised when God calls out our subtle lie or half-truth?

But even when we find that Jesus knows everything about the Samaritan woman, Jesus surprises us by not condemning her, but offering her life!

It's a paradox even the Samaritan woman didn't understand. She wants a life full of joy that will never end. And it's Jesus Himself that He offers to her — His very life and mercy.

This Samaritan woman, who was on her sixth man at this point, who had bought into the lie of giving up her dignity and her desire for intimate, true, and real relationship with a husband, was being offered everlasting life from one man, and His name is Jesus.

This is the paradox that Jesus offers us. He knows our life. He knows our sin. And He knows what we intimately desire. We feel so far from Him and we think He doesn't understand us. But what we find is Jesus who speaks truth into our lives and gives us a life that will never end in Him. It is Jesus Himself that brings everlasting life. It is our life in His life that brings us to our eternal freedom that we all desire.

A PERSONAL CHALLENGE

Find someone you know that doesn't seem very lively and share with them one way Jesus brings you joy.

MONDAY

MARCH 24, 2014

GOSPEL
Luke 4:24-30

REFLECTION

Truth is a difficult thing. It's normal to want to hear the truth, but often nothing is more challenging to hear. We often desire to speak truth, but this can cause quite a bit of discomfort.

In this passage, Jesus is speaking truth from the Scriptures about the prophets His audience would have known so well. But Jesus put a very specific perspective on the truth He was speaking. He was making clear that it was Gentiles that were sometimes more open to the prophets of old. His point was that He was in their midst, proclaiming the Kingdom of God, and they were rejecting Him. That was too challenging for the people of His hometown to hear, and they were driven to anger.

It is not our role to anger or upset people — it is our role to proclaim and listen to truth, even when it is difficult or inconvenient. Even if the truth angers or upsets people, we are called to share it... but with love. We are called to be proclaimers of the Kingdom of God, and to do so like Christ did: with love and compassion.

A PERSONAL CHALLENGE

Pray for the courage to boldly speak God's truth. Ask God to give you His wisdom and understanding, along with the willingness to share the truth of Christ with love.

TUESDAY

MARCH 25, 2014

GOSPEL
Luke 1:26-38

REFLECTION

This Gospel is a familiar story. An angel visits Mary and tells her that she will have a son, by the Holy Spirit, and that He will be called the Son of God. It's hard to imagine what Mary must have felt in that moment. Did she experience fear and confusion or wonder and amazement? Since she had a prayer life and a relationship with God, she knew that she could ask God how it was logically even possible. Mary trusted God and His answer. God showed her that He was in control and Mary not only trusted

Him with the small things, but she trusted God with *everything*.

There may be situations in your life that seem impossible. An upcoming algebra test, a broken friendship, or a sick family member. Mary wasn't afraid to ask God a question and she also wasn't afraid to trust in His answers. Do you ask God to tell you His will and His promises for your life? Do you trust in His answers when He does?

A PERSONAL CHALLENGE

In exciting or difficult times, it may be your first instinct to ask the question, "Why?" Write down one of these situations in your life and instead ask God how He will work in it or be glorified through it.

WEDNESDAY

GOSPEL
Matthew 5:17-19

REFLECTION

As history would tell us, change is going to come. There are thousands of history books filled with countless stories of empires rising and falling, of kings coming and going, and of groups of people moving from this land to that land. Even nowadays we try to make things our own and change whatever we can in a search for some kind of individuality and truth.

Change is an unavoidable part of life, however it's not always met with open arms. The beautiful part of Jesus' message in this Gospel is that He knew that. He came to *fulfill* the law rather than change it completely and start over. Jesus recognized the beauty and importance of what was, and fulfilled the laws that were already in place by His life, death, and Resurrection.

A PERSONAL CHALLENGE

Reflect upon your own "laws" in your life that you encounter. These might include respecting your parents, doing chores, or being a good sibling. Next time you feel resistance towards living into these "laws," offer up a prayer for your family and joyfully embrace the situation.

THURSDAY

MARCH 27, 2014

GOSPEL
Luke 11:14-23

REFLECTION
Do we trust that Jesus has the power to heal us? I think it is easy to answer a quick "yes" to this question, but do we allow this belief to affect the way we respond to the trials we encounter in our daily lives? In this Gospel passage, the people question the authority in which Jesus has the ability to heal. Knowing their innermost thoughts, Jesus warns them, "He who is not with me is against me, and whoever does not gather with me scatters" (Matthew 12:30).

Jesus desires that we have an unwavering trust in Him. Though our faith is not always perfect and we tend to doubt Jesus like those in the passage, He is not any less capable of delivering us to salvation.

Jesus has a heart of compassion and only calls us to unite ourselves to Him in our brokenness because He knows He is our only way to eternal life. When we choose to say, "Jesus I trust You and You are all that matters," any sort of doubt, anxiety, or fear in our daily lives is brought to the light to be healed.

A PERSONAL CHALLENGE

Write down three concerns that you have been struggling with this week. In prayer, offer up your concerns and entrust Jesus in His power to heal you, expressing that He is *all* that matters in your journey to eternal life.

FRIDAY

MARCH 28, 2014

GOSPEL

Mark 12:28-34

REFLECTION

This Gospel passage is commonly referred to as the parable of the Greatest Commandment. A scribe (a scholar of the law) asks Jesus which commandment is the greatest. Jesus answers: To love God with our entire being and to love others. Jesus says that there is nothing more important than doing these two things. Everything good falls under these two commandments, including all other commandments. Sin affects both God and neighbor, and thus, breaks them both. Focus your thoughts, words, feelings, and actions on pleasing the Lord. If we do that, loving the people in our lives will come naturally.

God is pleased when we love others and treat them with the dignity that He created them with. When you mess up, head to the Sacrament of Reconciliation so you can start over living out the Greatest Commandment.

A PERSONAL CHALLENGE

Love others by putting them first: smile at the kid no one talks to at school, hold a door open for someone even if you have to wait a few extra seconds for them to get to it or choose to be last for something.

SATURDAY

GOSPEL
Luke 18:9-14

REFLECTION
Jesus tells us in this passage that "everyone who exalts himself will be humbled, and the one who humbles himself will be exalted" (Luke 18:14). Now that sounds nice, but what does it really mean?

It often seems we need to be perfect to be exalted. After all, the people who get awards at school are the smartest, the fastest, or the best at something. Sometimes it can feel like we have to do the same thing in the Christian life. We have to be better than that one sin, we need to have perfect attendance at youth group, or to be the perfect Christian.

Today's Gospel helps us see the way God sees. In the parable, the Pharisee goes to prayer listing off all the things he does "right." Then, a tax collector comes and simply prays, "O, God be merciful to me" (Luke 18:13). Jesus points to the tax collector, not the Pharisee, as the example for His followers. He shows us the way to be exalted — to be honest with Him about our sins and seek His mercy. If we do that, God will exalt us and lift us up out of our sin.

A PERSONAL CHALLENGE

Lent is a great time to be honest with the Lord about our sins. If you haven't been to Confession in a while, find a day this week to go.

FOURTH WEEK
OF LENT

FOURTH SUNDAY OF LENT

MARCH 30, 2014

READING I
1 Samuel 16:1b, 6-7, 10-13a

READING II
Ephesians 5:8-14

GOSPEL

As Jesus passed by he saw a man blind from birth. He spat on the ground and made clay with the saliva, and smeared the clay on his eyes, and said to him, "Go wash in the Pool of Siloam" — which means Sent. So he went and washed, and came back able to see.

His neighbors and those who had seen him earlier as a beggar said, "Isn't this the one who used to sit and beg?" Some said, "It is," but others said, "No, he just looks like him." He said, "I am."

They brought the one who was once blind to the Pharisees. Now Jesus had made clay and opened his eyes on a sabbath. So then the Pharisees also asked him how he was able to see. He said to them, "He put clay on my eyes, and I washed, and now I can see."

So some of the Pharisees said, "This man is not from God, because he does not keep the sabbath." But others said, "How can a sinful man do such signs?" And there was a division among them. So they said to the blind man again, "What do you have to say about him, since he opened your eyes?" He said, "He is a prophet."

They answered and said to him, "You were born totally in sin, and are you trying to teach us?" Then they threw him out.

When Jesus heard that they had thrown him out, he found him and said, "Do you believe in the Son of Man?" He answered and said, "Who is he, sir, that I may believe in him?" Jesus said to him, "You have seen him, and the one speaking with you is he." He said, "I do believe, Lord," and he worshiped him.

- John 9:1, 6-9, 13-17, 34-38

REFLECTION

Jesus Christ proclaims that He is the "light of the world" and the Gospel tells the story of a man who was born blind, in darkness, and was given the gift of sight, to see the light. His eyes were opened in the simple but symbolic act of Christ spitting on dirt and anointing the blind man's eyes. This act of love reflects the original creation of man. So what is Jesus doing here? He is making a new creation.

After the blind man receives his sight something very interesting happens, no one believes him. The Pharisees and the people make up countless excuses that could explain what happened in every possible way rather than admitting that Jesus Christ is the Son of God.

We, too, are like the blind man, for each of us was born into darkness and blindness by original sin. But in the great gift of Baptism we are washed clean and made new creations in Christ. Our eyes and hearts are open to the graces of salvation, and we are able to see the light of Christ, which guides us to eternal life.

But how often is this enough for us? How often do we ask more of God in order to believe? He has given us everything, yet we find ourselves praying for that one more sign to prove it all. Are we blind to all the wondrous deeds He has already done for us? Do we find ourselves acting like the Pharisees, looking for every other explanation and living our lives skeptical of the reality of what Christ has done for us?

Christ has opened your eyes; He has washed the darkness away and brought you into the light. "Today, when you hear his voice, do not harden your hearts" (Hebrews 3:7-8), but rather open your eyes to the wonders that God is working in your life. Be like the blind man and fall at the feet of Christ and proclaim, "Lord, I believe"!

A PERSONAL CHALLENGE

Write down ten things in your life that you are
thankful for, and ten ways that you have seen God
work in your life. If you can't come up with ten, start
with five. If you are "blind" to even five, just focus
on one and start there. Thank God for the little ways
that He has revealed His love to you and pray for
your eyes to always be open to see His great light in
all ways, every day.

MONDAY

MARCH 31, 2014

GOSPEL
John 4:43-54

REFLECTION

Time and time again, Jesus grants signs to people
who believe before seeing. In this passage, the man
who approached Jesus to ask for his son's healing
"believed what Jesus said to him" (John 4:50). Because
of the man's faith, his son was healed and "his whole
household came to believe" (John 4:53).

God is calling us to believe *before* we see. We are
asked to pray without knowing completely how God

will respond. We are asked to love others without knowing how they will respond. We are asked to follow God without knowing what lies ahead.

The more we believe in Him, the more we live for Him; the more we live for Him, the more we believe in Him.

Since, "unless [we] see signs and wonders, [we] will not believe" (John 4:48), God gives us one sign that is greater than any other. The greatest sign of His love is His life poured out on the cross. The greatest sign of His power is His rising from the dead.

A PERSONAL CHALLENGE

Find a quiet area and read the story of Christ's passion found in John 18:28-20:31. Reflect on the sign that Christ offered when He gave His life for us and pray for the grace to allow His Resurrection to be a sufficient sign for your belief.

TUESDAY

APRIL 1, 2014

GOSPEL
John 5:1-16

REFLECTION

In this Gospel, we can think of the sick man as ourselves in a sinful state. Lost and alone, at the end of our strength, this passage shows us how we don't have to do anything except rely on Christ. Jesus is never too busy for grace and salvation, and He gives it freely. He meets us where we are, and all we need to do is receive. Receive His love, mercy, and healing.

Perhaps most important is what we do with His love. This passage shows us that Jesus will not leave us. Even as others admonish us as we speak of how Jesus works in our life, He gives us continued strength to proclaim His name.

A PERSONAL CHALLENGE

Find one blessing the Lord bestowed upon you and share it with someone.

WEDNESDAY

APRIL 2, 2014

GOSPEL
John 5:17-30

REFLECTION

In this Gospel, Jesus teaches us obedience. All Jesus was doing was what He was sent to do: Obey His Father who sent Him. Jesus speaks truth to us; He teaches us to stand up for what we believe. He teaches us that following Him includes persecution and being frowned upon by those who don't fully understand our faith.

He invites us to grow closer to Him (being both divine and human) and reveals to us His power: the power to judge the living and the dead and warns us of the consequences.

Finally, He reminds us that everything we do, must be in accordance with what He has sent us to do.

A PERSONAL CHALLENGE

List some areas God is asking you to grow in. Choose one and follow through with it today. No matter how big or how small.

THURSDAY

APRIL 3, 2014

GOSPEL
John 5:31-47

REFLECTION
This Gospel challenges us to look at whom we are serving. For Jesus says He can do nothing on His own, that He can only carry out orders as a servant does from His Master. From this point of servant, there is fullness of life and a fullness of joy. Not a list of do's and do not's, but a purpose of living for the Father no matter if crowd approval follows or if He is standing alone.

What does our life say to others? Are we pointing those around us to the living God or are we pointing them to ourselves? Does our presence in a room bring the peace and joy of Christ?

A PERSONAL CHALLENGE
Take time throughout the day to seek God's will and be obedient to His voice. Maybe it is sitting next to someone new in the lunchroom or maybe it is a simple as smiling at someone in the hallway. Pray that the Lord would give you His eyes and ears to better

"see" and hear the needs of the souls around you.
Whatever God speaks, be quick to answer in joyful
obedience.

FRIDAY

APRIL 4, 2014

GOSPEL
John 7:1-2, 10, 25-30

REFLECTION
Christ calls us to proclaim the Gospel at all times.
Not simply when we feel like it, or just when it is
convenient, or only when it is easy, but all the time.

In this Gospel Jesus goes to Judea and speaks publicly,
fully aware that there were people that would hear
Him speak who wished to arrest and kill Him. He
spoke with authority and without fear of persecution
and He calls us to do the same. When we speak the
truth to others we must speak with confidence and
without fear of what others might think or how they
may react.

This may be easier said than done, but take courage
that God will always be with you and protect you.
At the end of this passage we see that God protected

LIFE TEEN

Jesus from arrest, saying His time had not yet come. Follow Christ's example — be bold and trust that God will always protect, guide, comfort, and love you unconditionally.

A PERSONAL CHALLENGE

Think of someone you know that is suffering through something difficult and come up with a way to courageously show God's love to them.

SATURDAY

APRIL 5, 2014

GOSPEL

John 7:40-53

REFLECTION

This Bible passage is part of a larger passage, where Jesus' teachings lead to tension between the crowd, who believes in Him, and the Pharisees, who don't. The Pharisees even send guards to arrest Him, but after hearing Jesus teach and speak truth into their hearts, the guards too believe in Him. When the Pharisees ask why they didn't bring back Jesus, they answer with a short, powerful testimony: "Never before has anyone spoken like this one" (John 7:46). Christ's words transformed their beliefs.

How often do we let Christ's words sink into our hearts and transform us? There is so much power in the truth! Truth resonates within our hearts; it makes us come alive and sets us free. It transforms us into courageous men and women, who stand up for justice and truth, who stand up for Christ! Those guards even spoke up against the Pharisees!

When we truly listen to Christ, by reading the Bible and praying, we can — like these guards — be people who dare to speak up for the truth. Speaking even to those who might respond with unbelief, like the Pharisees. People are in desperate need of knowing the truth, so don't be afraid to share it.

A PERSONAL CHALLENGE

Be courageous today and share Christ's truth with someone who does not believe in Jesus. Share your faith with them.

FIFTH WEEK
OF LENT

FIFTH SUNDAY OF LENT

APRIL 6, 2014

READING I
Ezekiel 37:12-14

READING II
Romans 8:8-11

GOSPEL

The sisters of Lazarus sent word to Jesus, saying, "Master, the one you love is ill." When Jesus heard this he said, "This illness is not to end in death, but is for the glory of God, that the Son of God may be glorified through it." Now Jesus loved Martha and her sister and Lazarus. So when he heard that he was ill, he remained for two days in the place where he was. Then after this he said to his disciples, "Let us go back to Judea."

When Jesus arrived, he found that Lazarus had already been in the tomb for four days. When Martha heard that Jesus was coming, she went to meet him; but Mary sat at home. Martha said to Jesus, "Lord, if you had been here, my brother would not have died. But even now I know that whatever you ask of God,

God will give you." Jesus said to her, "Your brother will rise." Martha said, "I know he will rise, in the resurrection on the last day." Jesus told her, "I am the resurrection and the life; whoever believes in me, even if he dies, will live, and everyone who lives and believes in me will never die. Do you believe this?" She said to him, "Yes, Lord. I have come to believe that you are the Christ, the Son of God, the one who is coming into the world."

He became perturbed and deeply troubled, and said, "Where have you laid him?" They said to him, "Sir, come and see." And Jesus wept. So the Jews said, "See how he loved him." But some of them said, "Could not the one who opened the eyes of the blind man have done something so that this man would not have died?"

So Jesus, perturbed again, came to the tomb. It was a cave, and a stone lay across it. Jesus said, "Take away the stone." Martha, the dead man's sister, said to him, "Lord, by now there will be a stench; he has been dead for four days." Jesus said to her, "Did I not tell you that if you believe you will see the glory of God?" So they took away the stone. And Jesus raised his eyes and said, "Father, I thank you for hearing me. I know that you always hear me; but because of the crowd here I have said this, that they may believe that you sent me." And when he had said this, He cried out in a loud voice, "Lazarus, come out!" The dead man came out, tied hand and foot with burial bands, and his face was wrapped in a cloth. So Jesus said to them, "Untie him and let him go."

Now many of the Jews who had come to Mary and seen what he had done began to believe in him.

- John 11:3-7, 20-27, 33b-45

REFLECTION

God loves to work miracles. Christ's miracles not only restore people to physical life and spiritual health, but also, restore them to their families and communities. In this Gospel story, we hear how Lazarus was dead for days before Jesus showed up on the scene and miraculously raised him from the dead.

Physical death is very much a reality in our lives today, but people can also experience spiritual death. When we sin, especially when we commit mortal sins and purposefully turn our backs to God, our souls are so separated from God that it's like a spiritual death (Romans 6:23). If we're not living in God's grace, we're not really living.

Just as God can bring anyone back from a physical death, He can also bring anyone back from a spiritual death. Jesus wants to reach out to you and say "rise" no matter how far down in the pit of sin you are; Jesus loves you no less than He loved His close friend Lazarus. Saint Josemaría Escrivá once said, *"Jesus is*

your friend. The Friend. With a human heart, like yours. With loving eyes that wept for Lazarus. And He loves you as much as He loved Lazarus."

Jesus is the only one who can bring someone back from the dead. No matter how much we love and care for our brothers and sisters in Christ, we cannot save them from sin. Sure, we are responsible to help each other get to heaven, but only God can bring new life to someone's soul. The best thing that we can do for ourselves and for others is to turn all of our brokenness over to God.

Lent is a time of purification. It's a time for us to look around our lives and get rid of the things that are bringing us further and further away from God's light. We need to purify ourselves of the things that drag us deeper into the darkness and death of sin. You don't have to do it alone though. Will you let Jesus bring you back to life?

A PERSONAL CHALLENGE
Get to Confession this week and allow God to bring new life to your soul.

MONDAY

APRIL 7, 2014

GOSPEL
John 8:1-11

REFLECTION

Could you imagine being publicly humiliated for your sin?

The Pharisees bring this woman to Jesus, put her in the middle of all of them, and ask Him to condemn her. Jesus' first response? He bends down and writes something in the sand. Some scholars debate as to what Jesus wrote while others believe the important part isn't what He wrote but that He saved the woman from shame and embarrassment. We see that His heart is bent towards restoring her dignity and inviting her back into a way of life that brings peace, joy, and freedom.

Jesus does the same for each of us when we veer off course. He doesn't approach us with condemnation, and His desire is not to shame or embarrass us. Instead, He confidently redirects our path of life and invites us to continue on.

A PERSONAL CHALLENGE

Spend a few minutes writing down the areas of your life where your sin has held you back from experiencing the peace, joy, and freedom that Jesus desires for you. Now reread John 8:1-11 and imagine Jesus writing you a personal message in the sand. What does it say? Journal about the meaning behind it.

TUESDAY

APRIL 8, 2014

GOSPEL
John 8:21-30

REFLECTION

Jesus calls the Pharisees out of their hypocritical judgments and challenges them to look inward. If they do not profess Him as Lord, they will perish in their sin.

Too often we live lives that are both heavenly **and** earthly. Attending Mass, saying the rosary, helping in various church activities, etc., are all good things. However, what happens when we're away from a religious environment? Magazines, television shows, movies, and music have an effect on who we are. They are not bad in and of themselves, but they can easily take the attention away from Christ, if we let it.

Appearances aren't everything. The Pharisees did everything "right" outwardly, but their hearts grew rigid with a worldly poison. The choices we make can lead us closer to heaven or not. And if we're not moving closer to heaven, we're moving toward hell. The choice is ours. Jesus calls us to fix our eyes on Him daily. Can we hear His call in the midst of so many distractions?

A PERSONAL CHALLENGE

Take some time today and ask Christ where in your life you've been living "of the world." Ask for the strength to change and make a firm resolution to stop watching that TV show, turn off that music... you know what it is.

WEDNESDAY

APRIL 9, 2014

GOSPEL
John 8:31-42

REFLECTION

Jesus says, "everyone who commits sin is a slave of sin" (John 8:34). That means that because we all commit sin, every one of us is a slave of sin. You may experience that slavery to sin when you commit the same sins over and over. The good news, though, is that it doesn't end there. Jesus does not leave us in our weakness. He is the Truth that can set us free from our slavery to sin.

Lent is a time to allow Christ to conquer our sins. We cannot do this by ourselves. Because we are slaves, we cannot set ourselves free. The power of Christ is the only thing that can set us free from the sin in our lives. Will you allow Him to do this for you? Do you want to be free?

As Catholics, we have the gift of the Sacrament of Reconciliation. Reconciliation gives us the opportunity to receive God's mercy and receive the grace we need to keep fighting the battle against sin. Sometimes it takes confessing the same sin over and over to find freedom in our lives, but Christ will bring us this freedom if we ask for it.

A PERSONAL CHALLENGE

Think of one specific sin that you feel enslaves you. This could be a sin that you commit often, or one that you confess often. Ask Jesus to free you from this sin. If you need to go to Confession, commit to going to Confession at the next available opportunity.

THURSDAY

APRIL 10, 2014

GOSPEL
John 8:51-59

REFLECTION

In today's Gospel, Jesus speaks about why we should follow God, and how we should follow Him. If we follow God, and keep His word, His plan for us, we will have eternal life. Then, we give all the glory, all the thanks to Him. It's really that simple.

So how do we know God's plan for us? Jesus says, "But I do know him and I keep his word" (John 8:55). Jesus prayed to God, and talked to God a lot, so that God could tell Him the next right step. If we want to know God's intentions for us and for our lives, we have to talk with Him every day. He will guide us, but we have to keep our ears tuned in to the Holy Spirit.

A PERSONAL CHALLENGE

Take some time in a quiet place today to talk to God. Just ask Him, "God, what do You want me to do today?"

FRIDAY

APRIL 11, 2014

GOSPEL

John 10:31-42

REFLECTION

When Jesus Christ walked the earth, there were multiple debates and disagreements about who He was. Jesus was a Jew, and Jews believed in one God. They believe that God sent prophets to earth to prepare the way for the Messiah. For centuries, the Jews were waiting for the Messiah to save their people, but you can imagine that they weren't eager to believe just any person who claimed to be the Messiah. Especially a humble guy like Jesus of Nazareth, a son of Joseph the carpenter. They expected that the Messiah would be a powerful king and ruler of the earth.

Here in John 10, Jesus is being confronted (yet again) for claiming to be the Son of God. Jesus, the Wise Teacher, would never jump foolishly into a debate. Instead, He challenged His fellow Jews and called them to take a close look at God the Father and His works. Only then would they see that God the Father and God the Son were one in the same. They didn't have to look very far because Jesus was performing inexplicable miracles throughout the region.

What's more logical? To dismiss a man who performs miracles as *crazy*, or to believe that this Great Healer is one with God? This question is as relevant today as it was 2000 years ago.

A PERSONAL CHALLENGE

Take some time to journal about who you think Jesus is. Do you live your life like He is your God, a distant friend, or a stranger? If you're not living like He is your God, write down some ways to improve your relationship with Him.

SATURDAY

APRIL 12, 2014

GOSPEL
John 11:45-56

REFLECTION

The prophecy of the high priest in today's Gospel sets the stage for Passion Sunday and Good Friday by reminding us why this all matters: It is better for one man to die rather than the entire nation. What the high priest did not know was that the one man about to die was wholly innocent and was going to take the punishment that we deserve.

It can be easy to forget this reality. We deserve death because of our sin, but because of the sacrifice of Christ on the cross we can be given eternal life. That is what the pain and suffering of the coming days is all about — love. We may listen to the Passion story and get distracted and stop listening, but what Jesus is about to do is the most important thing that could happen. His death will mean our life. Think about that: Jesus loves us so much that He would give Himself up so that we all could live. You are worth the price of His blood.

A PERSONAL CHALLENGE

Write out Romans 6:23, "For the wages of sin is death, but the gift of God is eternal life in Christ Jesus our Lord," and tape it to your bathroom mirror. Pray it every morning and remember it, especially during Holy Week.

HOLY
WEEK

PALM SUNDAY

APRIL 13, 2014

READING I
Isaiah 50:4-7

READING II
Philippians 2:6-11

GOSPEL
Matthew 26:14-27 - 27:66

(Go ahead and look up this verse and read it.)

REFLECTION

The same crowds who shout "Hosanna," will soon be shouting, "crucify Him." The same Peter that promises he will not abandon Christ will soon deny Him three times. The disciples, who saw all Christ did and heard all that He taught, will abandon Him and scatter in fear.

Jesus dies for them anyway.

Imagine being Christ as all this is happening. What kind of love would it take to still sacrifice your life for these people? We hold grudges so easily and get mad if we hear someone gossiping behind our back. We get angry if we don't get a text back right away. But to be denied and abandoned? Totally betrayed? It would be hard to love people who did that to us.

We may not have been physically there that Good Friday, but Christ knew our sins as He prayed in the garden. He sweat blood in agony over the times that we would choose sin and fear over His love. He knew that we would be just like the other disciples who turned and abandoned Him out of fear. He knew that we would be like Peter, and we would deny Him before others, even when we promise not to.

He knew that we would be just like the crowd that shouted, "crucify Him" and then chose a murderous rebel to free instead of the King of kings when Pilate offered them the choice. Jesus knew that there are times we are going to choose sin over life, rebellion instead of our Lord. Even when we shout, "Crucify Him." Jesus simply responds, "I love you and forgive you," as He stretches out His hands to be nailed to a cross.

That is the love Christ has for us, even in our sinfulness, even though we are the ones who nail Him to the cross.

What did we do to deserve such a savior? We sinned, and God loved us beyond that. This week we will watch as we see the lengths that love will go for the beloved, the lengths that Christ will go for the people who hand Him over to death, turn their back on Him, and deny Him.

Christ loved you anyway.

A PERSONAL CHALLENGE

Despite our sin, Christ loves us and forgives us. This week write a letter to someone that you need to forgive, or forgive him or her in person.

MONDAY OF HOLY WEEK

APRIL 14, 2014

GOSPEL
John 12:1-11

REFLECTION
It's easy to feel pretty good about ourselves when we go to church and others do not. There's a subtle trap that occurs when we begin to think we are somehow "holier" than our peers because we "know Jesus" better than they might.

Judas knew Jesus, too. He was not only a follower and disciple, he was included in the band of the Lord's very closest followers. He was present at countless unrecorded moments, never seen in a Gospel, where Jesus undoubtedly shared intimate and striking insight into the Kingdom of heaven and the Father's love… and, yet, Judas still did what he did. He may have thought himself somehow "superior" to others; Judas may have thought himself holier than other sinners given how close he had become to Jesus. Those on the outside looking in would have definitely seen Judas as "close" to Jesus, not realizing how far his heart was moving in the opposite direction. Judas may have spoken about loving the poor but it was Mary, in her act of service, that demonstrated her own poverty of spirit. In anointing Christ's feet, Mary left little doubt as to how she loved or Whom she loved. Mary's action proclaimed more about her holiness than any words Judas (or we) could ever use. This day, strive to be like Mary who focused on her love for Jesus not other's (apparent) lack of it.

A PERSONAL CHALLENGE

Open your Bible to this passage from John chapter 12. Once you find the page, mark it and then say a prayer, asking the Holy Spirit to open your eyes and heart in a new way. Then, reread this Gospel passage a couple more times. Each time you read the account, write out a word or phrase that jumps out at you. Look for details and adjectives, images, and visuals and record each of them. Picture the room. Smell the oil. Envision the faces. Hear the inflection in each voice. Ask the Holy Spirit why the words you recorded were included and why they struck a chord in your heart. Entering into the story more fully each day will ensure that this is not "just another Holy Week."

TUESDAY OF HOLY WEEK

APRIL 15, 2014

GOSPEL
John 13:21-33, 36-38

REFLECTION
In Judas and Peter we have two very different approaches yet both will end in betrayal. Judas intends to sin, but Peter contends with it. Judas' plan is clear and the plot is set in motion. Jesus, aware of what is transpiring, does not stand in the way. Our Lord is also aware, however, of how Peter's proclamation of faith and fidelity will end with the cock's crow. Although both will let Jesus down in their discipleship this night, only one intended to do

so (Judas). Peter may have failed in his pursuit but at least his intentions were pure as the night drew near.

Sin doesn't just spontaneously happen. Sin is a decision on our part. Sometimes it is something we plan to do, after justifying it to ourselves (Judas) and sometimes it is something we choose in the moment due to fear (like Peter) or selfishness or pride. The good news is that in the end, Jesus loved both Judas and Peter the same — even knowing their choices and shortcomings — Jesus' love for each man was perfect. God didn't love Judas and Peter differently, it was Judas and Peter who loved God differently. Sin reveals who we love more (God or ourselves) at any given moment and our repentance (or lack thereof) reveals who we love more in the moments that follow.

A PERSONAL CHALLENGE

Take some time to reflect on the situations, locations, and relationships that most often lead you into sin. You know the dangers that each present, so be honest with yourself and with God. Do you actively choose these moments, knowing full well that you might sin? Do you seek sin and seek to justify that sin like Judas? How about the times you think yourself stronger than you really are and end up sinning, like Peter? How could you have handled those situations differently? Spend a solid 20 minutes praying and asking God for

the strength to avoid sin and, when you fall, to seek
His mercy in the Sacrament of Reconciliation.

WEDNESDAY OF HOLY WEEK

APRIL 16, 2014

GOSPEL
Matthew 26:14-25

REFLECTION

It's easy to honor God with our words and then
abandon Him in our thoughts and actions. It's easy
to claim that Jesus is our Lord but then deny Him
with our lifestyle. Notice that the eleven — when
discussing who the betrayer was — all referred to
Jesus as "Lord" but when his turn came, Judas did
not.

"Surely it is not I, Rabbi?" the betrayer responded.

Why didn't Judas call Jesus "Lord" like the rest of
the apostles? What was different in his heart that
prevented him from addressing Jesus as his Lord?
Notice in the Lord's response, too, that it wasn't Jesus
who condemned Judas but, really, Judas who had

condemned himself by his own decisions, his deal with the chief priests, and his ensuing action. Judas' response to God is one of those seemingly "minor" details that is easily missed, but when contemplated in prayer, it opens our eyes to a much deeper reality. We are all called to the table of the Lord, but how we approach that table makes all the difference.

A PERSONAL CHALLENGE

Ponder this prayer, "I love You, Jesus. Thank You for loving me. You and You alone are my Lord and my Savior."

Write it out in your own handwriting. Write it over and over again. Commit it to memory. Tonight, head to bed 30 minutes early and pray only this prayer. Pray it slowly and intentionally. Consider each word. Which part of the prayer is most comforting and which is most challenging to pray and mean? Reflect on what you are saying and whether or not your heart's inclinations match your lips profession. Spend some time in silence, asking the Lord to reveal to you what you need to do differently as you move into this most holy weekend.

EASTER
TRIDUUM

HOLY THURSDAY - MASS OF THE LORD'S SUPPER

APRIL 17, 2014

GOSPEL
John 13:1-15

REFLECTION

We've all heard the story of Christ washing the feet of His apostles. In fact, we've probably heard it so many times that it can begin to lose its impact. How crazy it is that an action like the Creator kneeling before His creation in such a humble posture can become so common and unexciting!

The God of the Universe isn't just loving them, He's showing how much He loves you! The One who died for you is showing you how He wants you to live! This is more than a nice act before a nice meal before Jesus has to leave… this is Jesus taking the gloves off, sounding an alarm and declaring a war on sin with the weapon of love. This is Jesus giving ALL Christians a new mission… to love Him through service of one another.

Note, too, when this action takes place within the Last Supper… it's before Jesus gives us the Eucharist. The order matters a great deal. We must understand our mission (to serve) before He gives us the power and grace (Eucharist) to accomplish it. The next time you go forward for communion, remember that He is giving you the love you need with an expectation for you to share it on the mission He has entrusted to you.

A PERSONAL CHALLENGE

Do everything you can to get to your parish tonight and enter into the Holy Thursday Mass and prayer time. There is no better way to celebrate what occurred in the upper room 2000 years ago than to visit the upper room in the sanctuary in your local Catholic Church. If for some reason you cannot go, create a prayerful space in your room or home. Light some candles, reread this passage, and thank God not only for the gift of His priesthood and His Eucharistic body and blood, but for inviting you into this mission of love and service by virtue of your Baptism.

GOOD FRIDAY

APRIL 18, 2014

GOSPEL
John 18:1 - 19:42

REFLECTION & CHALLENGE

Take your own Bible and read through the passage listed above. Say a prayer, first, asking the Holy Spirit to guide you through it. Pay attention to details you may have never noticed before. Ask the Lord to open your eyes to the moments and words where He wishes to conflict or comfort your soul. Take in each scene. When you read a piece of dialogue, consider how it would have sounded that day. Pause frequently and thank the Lord for what He went through.

After reading through it, invite the Blessed Virgin Mary to kneel beside you and pray with you. Ponder how she felt watching the events unfold and consider the amount of trust that the Blessed Mother must have had to be able to endure such heartache. Spend some time in silence and allow her prayer to comfort you on this holy day.

HOLY SATURDAY

APRIL 19, 2014

GOSPEL

In observance of Holy Saturday, there is no Gospel reading for the day.

REFLECTION & CHALLENGE

Spend some time praying for all of those souls who will be entering into the Church at the Easter Vigil — either through Baptism or a Profession of Faith. Take time, too, to thank God for all of those people who have been examples of faithfulness to you and for those who have handed the faith on to you. Call a parent or grandparent and thank them for their example. Post on someone's Facebook page or Twitter feed thanking them for sharing Christ's light with the world. Demonstrate your appreciation for those who have proudly lived for God, and beg God for the courage to do the same every day of your life until He calls you home to heaven.

EASTER SUNDAY

APRIL 20, 2014

READING I
Acts 10:34a, 37-43

READING II
Colossians 3:1-4 or 1 Corinthians 5:6b-8

GOSPEL

On the first day of the week, Mary of Magdala came to the tomb early in the morning, while it was still dark, and saw the stone removed from the tomb. So she ran and went to Simon Peter and to the other disciple whom Jesus loved, and told them, "They have taken the Lord from the tomb, and we don't know where they put him." So Peter and the other disciple went out and came to the tomb. They both ran, but the other disciple ran faster than Peter and arrived at the tomb first; he bent down and saw the burial cloths there, but did not go in. When Simon Peter arrived after him, he went into the tomb and saw the burial cloths there, and the cloth that had covered his head, not with the burial cloths but rolled up in a separate place. Then the other disciple also went in, the one who had arrived at the tomb first, and he

saw and believed. For they did not yet understand the
Scripture that he had to rise from the dead.

- John 20:1-9

REFLECTION & CHALLENGE

Notice how much Mary and the apostles desired to
be with Jesus. Mary arrived before daybreak. The
apostles literally ran to hopefully see Him. They lived
with passion and with a sense of urgency.

Don't wait to celebrate Jesus' life. Talk with Him and
about Him. Share about Him. Post about Him. Sing
about Him. Laugh with Him. Cry with Him. Work on
a 30 second answer as to why Jesus is so important
to you and share it often when someone sees your
T-shirt or your cross or hears that you go to church.
You are called to be a living witness, not just on
Sundays or on Easter but *every single hour of every
single day* — that's what it means to be a Catholic
Christian and that is how we ensure that Easter is
never forgotten!

SPECIAL THANKS

WE'D LIKE TO THANK ALL THOSE WHO CONTRIBUTED TO THIS RESOURCE:

Anna Albert
Lazer Arreola
Mark Bocinsky
Amanda Cassar
Joe Chernowski
Stacy Cretors
Marlo Dowdy
Kevin Fenter
Jon Givens
Lizzie Gormley
Amanda Grubbs
Mark Hart
Rachel Huber
Asia-Lyn James
Jessica Lenehan
Stephen Lenahan
Jen Mason

Christina Mead
Nina Mertens
Ryan Miller
Ryan O'Connell
Casey Olson
Emily Pellarin
Zach Raus
Jordan Raus
Randy Raus
Leigh Anne Sanford
Nate Schaff
Matt Smith
Joel Stepanek
Natalie Tansill
Ginny Taylor
Sara Vasile
Pam Zimmerman

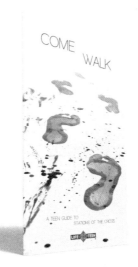

Come Walk
A Teen Guide to Stations of the Cross

The Stations of the Cross are a powerful invitation to follow Christ through His Passion and Death into Resurrection. *Come Walk: A Teen Guide to Stations of the Cross* helps extend that invitation to young people. Through simple explanations on how to pray this devotion and teen-friendly reflections on each Station, this small book can help lead both teens and adults closer to Christ and the salvation won for us on the cross.

Booklet stapled, 3.5"x5.5", 48 pages, **$3.00**
Also available in Spanish

Full of Grace
A Teen Guide to the Rosary

Make the rosary come alive in your own life with *Full of Grace: A Teen Guide to the Rosary*. Written for any soul wanting to grow closer to Christ and His mother; *Full of Grace* will not only teach you how to pray the rosary, but also guide you into a daily prayer routine with the rosary. As you pray with *Full of Grace*, you'll be drawn into the story of each mystery of the rosary through relatable and intimate reflections, perfect for all ages. Transform your prayer life today with *Full of Grace: A Teen Guide to the Rosary*.

Paperback, 3.5"x5.5", 92 pages, **$4.00**